Praise For The House Of Gathering

"Using words as wands, the wildly talented artist, performer, visionary, mystic and magic maker, Erica Sarzin-Borrillo offers a feast of life in all its stages and surprises. Here is truth telling wrought in poetic images and stunning cadence. The Goddess takes up residence in this potent book and the reader is never the same".

-Jean Houston, *Ph.D., author of "The Possible Human"*

"Erica Sarzin-Borrillo invites us on a metaphysical journey of self-discovery, one that we must undertake, despite its emotional and spiritual perils. In her guided passage, she encourages us to cast away the pretentions of self and set sail with universal truth, which delivers us to the far shore."

–Robert Bows, *pseudonymous author of "Solomon's Proof."*

"Erica Sarzin-Borrillo's stunning book, The House of Gathering will be an enormous gift to anyone who reads it—as it will not only engage, but enlighten well beyond the imagination. She guides us through an auspicious journey into the mysteries of being alive in our time. It is written with such gentle grace while still soundly definitive in content with a sweeping poetic style—a genuine celebration of the significance of being PRESENT in life while being alive."

—Wayne Adams, *theatre producer, New York City*

"Erica Sarzin-Borrillo's mystical poetry awakens us to our divine essence. It inspires, consoles, and invites us to come home to the Eternal Lover, and be the resurrection of this world. As with the passionate verses of Hafiz and Rumi, here is expression of the ecstatic love affair, rich with depth, humor, mystery and inspiration. This is poetry, which is not created or manufactured, but birthed. In The House of Gathering you will experience fire, longing, benediction, and forgiveness, and you will want to plunge into these inviting depths again and again...."

-Jane Smith Bernhardt, author of We Are Here:
love never dies, and The Sweet Conversation:
a guide to spiritual listening

"Ms. Sarzin-Borrillo has a most extraordinary gift of describing the soul's journey and her poetry comes closer to expressing it than any writing I have ever experienced. Each piece is like looking at one of a thousand lights of the soul, each stimulating an inner sense that brings us closer to the truth of our own essence. We are lifted on word-wings that guide us inward to the awakening of our own Soul-Self. This poetry jump-starts that inner journey for those who have forgotten and for those who need reminding."

-Robert Stempson, co-author of "The Sixth Sense",
Founder and Director of PHD/Programs for
Human Development and ctpsychics.com.

The House of Gathering

The House of Gathering

ERICA SARZIN-BORRILLO

BALBOA.
PRESS
A DIVISION OF HAY HOUSE

Balboa Press books may be ordered through booksellers or by contacting:

Balboa Press
A Division of Hay House
1663 Liberty Drive
Bloomington, IN 47403
www.balboapress.com
1 (877) 407-4847

Because of the dynamic nature of the Internet, any web addresses or links contained in this book may have changed since publication and may no longer be valid. The views expressed in this work are solely those of the author and do not necessarily reflect the views of the publisher, and the publisher hereby disclaims any responsibility for them.

The author of this book does not dispense medical advice or prescribe the use of any technique as a form of treatment for physical, emotional, or medical problems without the advice of a physician, either directly or indirectly. The intent of the author is only to offer information of a general nature to help you in your quest for emotional and spiritual well-being. In the event you use any of the information in this book for yourself, which is your constitutional right, the author and the publisher assume no responsibility for your actions.

Any people depicted in stock imagery provided by Thinkstock are models, and such images are being used for illustrative purposes only. Certain stock imagery © Thinkstock.

Print information available on the last page.

ISBN: 978-1-4525-1686-8 (sc)
ISBN: 978-1-4525-1688-2 (hc)
ISBN: 978-1-4525-1687-5 (e)

Library of Congress Control Number: 2014910730

Balboa Press rev. date: 9/9/2014

This book is dedicated to Madeline Bayer,
Paul J. Curtis, and Wayne Adams:
My Mother, my teacher, my friend

The poets have scattered you
A storm ripped through the stammering
I want to gather you up again
In a vessel that makes you glad

I wander in a thousand winds
That you are churning
And bring back everything I find

The blind man needed you as a cup
The beggar held you out as I passed
You see, I am one who likes to look for things

I am one who barely noticed
Like a shepherd comes up from behind

One who dreams of making you complete
And in that way completes himself

Rainer Maria Rilke

Contents

Preface .... *xvii*

Higher Spirit – Authentic Soul

A Thousand Portraits..3

Spiral Dance...4

Everyman 5

The Ancient Future 6

Threads of Light..7

Soul to Soul 8

Contemplating Evolution 10

The Lonely Hunter 11

Inspiration Says...12

Poets 13

The Spirit of Loneliness...14

Dark Blessings 16

Embracing the Divine Feminine

Evolution..21

Just a Touch Away..22

The Goddess 24

The Bounty..26

Blessed Child 27

Mother..28

Mothers and Sons 30

Gaia Speaks 32

The Original Wound.. 35

Empress 36

Picasso's Children..38

My Name 40

Beloved Rendezvous

The Heavenly Dreams.. 45

Lighthouse 46

Beloved 47

Gratitude 48

Forever Young 50

Cosmic Lover...52

The Final Dance 54

The House of Gathering 56

Arms Wide Open in
The House of Longing

For Eons 65

I Am a Miner 66

Ohas Dancing 68

The Artist..70

Yearning 71

My Soul's Prayer 72

Passion 74

Get Soul..75

Hunger 76

Without You 78

Dreams 80

Mythic Voyages in the Tides of Change

Mandala 85

Beyond Eternity 86

Ancient Heroine 87

Land of Lot 88

The Lonely Journey 91

Destiny Finds Us 92

L' Destiny 94

Taking the Leap 96

Embracing the Paradox...98

Sea of Change 99

Hope Springs..100

Against the Odds...102

Why Not?..104

The Eternal Flame..106

Softening 108

World Wounding..110

Embracing Eternity

Hallelujah 115
My Mortality 116
Old Folks 118
Winter Days 120
Woman in the Mirror...122
Gathering the One..124
House of Mirrors...126
The Devil Laughs 128
One More Mission 129
Freedom 130
Surrender 132
Grieving 134
What Does the Universe Want from Me?....................136
The Masterpiece 138
The Usher..140
Will You Know Me? 141
Temple Dream 142

Acknowledgements 147
About the Author 149

Illustrations

Interior artwork for chapters by Erica Sarzin-Borrillo
Front cover sculpture, "Yule Mama" by Angela Treat Lyon

Preface

We reach into the abstract to give it form. We who are poets and artists alike inevitably struggle to bring into existence some sort of being out of that which is non-being in the gathering of Spirit and Soul. It is the way of all creation. Perhaps the very meaning of one's life begins with the deep urge to express the inexplicable. Art is the communication of Spirituality and the Soul's truth, which is eternally unfolding and coming to light out of Mysteries unknown. Walking hand in hand with the muse, we make our offerings to the Spirit of Beauty. For its only want is to reveal itself in the world as I, dear reader, make this offering to you. May we gather the very best of our lives and gather together as One.

Erica Sargin-Borrillo

Higher Spirit – Authentic Soul

Through the Veils

A Thousand Portraits

There are a thousand portraits to be painted

Before the Soul's essence can be captured

The tale of the one and the many

Is told a thousand different ways

While we work out our lives

So infinitely paradoxical

There are a thousand myths

Of the traveling fool

And what stands beneath his unique face

Is the face of Man

And behind the face of Man

Is the portrait of God Himself

Spiral Dance

A Spiral Dance began… but when?
There is no beginning…There is no end
The journey goes on as we search
For truth within illusions
And cling to the make believe
For the ego's sake…The little one
Who needs to believe in something!
Our Hearts long for you through it all
Perhaps you want us to tell you of our tales
And deliver new stories from far and wide
The circle of life widens
With each man's experience
But lifetime after lifetime
We become more distracted
Fooled by the Virtual and untrue
For to live one's life in denial
Is to live a life unlived
What has become of the Original Soul?
Who will even remember the name:
Human Being, given to us so very long ago?
I ask for Peace and once again turn within
To find my own Divinity
For this Life asks to be lived
With such an aliveness
That it borders on Ecstasy!
We talk of Evolution
But perhaps we first must return
To the Land of the Ancients
And bring back what's primal and True

Everyman

If you could only see your soul
Or at the very least feel it and express it
You would know
In the depths of your being
Your Holiness

You would recognize your Sacred bond
With The Soul of the world
The notion of being lost and alone
Would be no more
Your perception of your separateness
Would be perceived as mere perception
And you would come to realize
In the deepest sense
That your original self lives eternally
In your original home

Stand in this moment
In the Center of time and space
Grounded here
By the hearth of humanity
You are the lotus in full bloom
The dreamer and the dream come true

You are Everyman
Yet as unique as anyone could possibly be

Revel now
You are the Soul of the world

The Ancient Future

The future was present
Here there and everywhere
Yet from this angle
This perspective
I have no awareness
Of the very next moment
For this present moment
Takes such focus
And demands my attention
But in my knowing Heart
Where the witness can
Give its attention at all times to all times
I am being told that
The future is already here
It stands alone as a mystery
Yet is as ancient as time itself
And not only because its Ancient seed
Was planted long ago
But because past, present, and future
Are gathered as one simultaneously
You and I, my friend are the
Ancient Holy Tribesmen
Dancing by the fire in the dead of night
We are the Original Ones who created
The pathway into the future
And the time travelers from
The distant future making
Their way back to their
Original Soul

Threads of Light

For ages now
The light
Would not be seen
For fear of some
Kind of nakedness
Amongst your kind

It took time
To leave one's armor behind
Even though you had already
Lost the game
You were meant to lose
All along

Your warrior's garb
Is now torn and tattered
Your chain maille is barely intact
Yet you still hang on
For some archaic "stance"

Can you not see
That the end game has come
And your Mission's no longer to fight
It's time to shed your threads of fear
And bare your threads of Light

Soul to Soul

There is a longing within Mankind
That cannot be erased with time
We long for the original touch of Mother
Her arms around us
The bond between us
Her knowing of our needs...
Her needing our needs
For that bond, that base
That human connection
Which we so rarely achieve
Yet long for forever more

Forests are connected
Through a brilliant root system
And though we are the One and the Many
How distanced we all feel from each other

We seem to vacillate
Between the need to belong to each other
And the need to belong to our self alone
But we long to belong, to bond, to connect

There is a word: "gluon"
It means the connection
Of substance to substance
Another word for "Soul"

Soul... it is that connecting force
The bond, the base
The string theory, the glue

One wonders why
We even need to continue
Searching for some unifying factor
When it is already there
Within our Hearts

Soul… it is that Sacred force
Of beings large and small
The Animals, Vegetables,
Trees, Planets, Insects
Higher consciousness
Or the lowest of them all

Soul….It's not that we have run dry of it
It's that it's lost its value
Our Souls were sold so long ago
That perhaps it's but a dim memory
That remains

Perhaps when we find it again
With it we'll find the best
Of our Humanity

Contemplating Evolution

$\mathcal{I}$ see the world and indeed myself
In the hub of the wheel
Spinning out to World Karma
And back into the crystalline Center
Where the Cross-Point embraces all as One
And shines as the brightest Star
And from that absolute center
There is an absolute Vision...
A Vision that sees all Eternity...
A Vision that holds all Eternity
In the present moment

A Vision so pungent with Divine electricity
That all things are possible
Including Love, Grace, and Global Healing...
And World Peace...

Such Vision is perhaps the Vision
Of the Eye of I AM

Therefore, to See is to create...
To See is to Be
The Brightest Star shining light
From within and without
So that even when WE
Spin out to the far edges of
The Great Mandala

WE are still in the Starlight
And expression of its Center

The Lonely Hunter

One's whole Life is an unfolding of the Self
Creating an open Heart for the Angel part
To bring forth its Light and its goodness

But it rarely reveals itself in the World
And in the marketplace
The Heart is but a lonely hunter
Hunting for the Soul of another

We go to Church
And sit amongst the many
Seeking the very same thing:
The reconnection to
The Divine

We sit together on mass, in mass
Listening to the man in the pulpit
Yet rarely do we even notice each other

Don't we know where the
Sacred One resides
Don't we know it lies within
The stranger we cannot
Bring ourselves to See

Inspiration Says

Inspiration says:
Say what's on your mind and in your Soul
You've been hiding from the World
Your tender self who wants only to heal
And be healed
That is what you came here for

If there was nothing within or without
In need of tending
Or if conflict or wounding did not exist
There would be no movement towards life

As long as you are Human
You will always look for the Human flaws
For the cracks and imperfections

Your Soul is hungry for the inner stuff
Like a hunter for that which needs Transformation

Poets

The artist's experience is a mystical one
Our muse flies in from the heavens
Soaring on the wings of the dove
Singing the songbird's song

When we remember to see
Through the eye of the Soul
Our connection to
The Infinite is stirred

Life ignites
And so do we
And so do our relationships
It is just that simple

It takes the right kind of thinking
Or the willingness to go for the gold
That appears every time we put
God's pen to paper
Or make something artful of a blank canvas
Or when we use the original language
Of our own soul

We are poets underneath our toughened skin
And little ego of the world
We are poets all of us
If only we would know

The Spirit of Loneliness

Let us not lose sight
Of the Soul's secret agenda
Heading on the path to Freedom
Heading like an arrow
To the Center of its Truth
It insists on surprising us
By pulling the ground
From beneath our feet
Why do we insist
On altering its course
When all it ever wanted
Was to gather itself
In the arms of the Highest
And transform World suffering
At the hand of our illusions

Sometimes it seems
Like we have all been abandoned
And we're meant to go it alone
And like the Gods of Creation
We have been driven to make something
Out of nothing for our company
For indeed it can be a lonely, lonely world

Perhaps the truth is that Spirit
Is actually waiting patiently for our call
Our invitation to come alive within us
And that Loneliness itself is such a Spirit
Knowing its only hope is to find its perfect host

Perhaps the Loneliness
Of The Universe itself
Needed our company
Wanted to be expressed..
Needed to be felt
And needed to be understood

Even the Spirit of Tragedy
Asks for its moment of glory
And though we judge such things
Our Souls take Spirit seriously
For all things are on a secret mission together
And serve each other
Despite our need to interfere

The Spirit of Loneliness
Entered our House eons ago
Perhaps it only wished for console
And a warm embrace
And its only chance for transformation
Was to finally be greeted with Grace

Dark Blessings

The Angel of Night
Enters like a secret friend
Wanting only to unravel the truth
Hidden within the shadows

He brings with him
His Dark Blessings
But we fear such gifts
With our lack of faith
In life itself

The Mystery asks us
To take this journey
Each step of the way
And embrace the process
With the understanding
That there is no right
And there is no wrong

There is nothing
But your Soul's breath
And passion for a Human experience

Full of joy and challenges alike
Full of hope and disappointment all at once
Full of doubt and fear
As well as conviction
Full of order
And full of chaos

With the ever present instinct
To seek balance
And our highest potential

Living with the confusions and illusions
And projections of Mankind
Our Genius is invited in

The ready-made Wise Man
The One within
Who goes by the name
I Am

Embracing the Divine Feminine

In the Arms of all the Great Mothers

Evolution

There is silence in the dark night
But you can hear the Higher voice
Beneath the cacophony

You will find your footing in the wood
For the North Star shines bright
And the lover is always there
To take your hand

The Great Mother
Will gather you in her arms
As secret gardeners till the soil

All shall be well
For seedlings love to grow
And life loves evolution

Just a Touch Away

Just beyond the threshold
Just beyond the veil
Just a touch away
Yet never truly attainable
Our ancient lover waits
She is the one the artists
Seek when they make
Form of the abstract
She is the one we seek
Yearning to fill our
Hearts in the city
Of empty dreams
Every day in every way
We strike our fellow man
And try as we may
To love, and be loved
As long as the ancient lover
Is lost and forgotten
All we can do is buy and sell
In the mall of illusion
The future of humankind
That is already upon us
Has come a long way
Such an infinitely long way
From our true nature
That one wonders why
The lover still waits

But there she is with open arms
You can see her just out
Of the corner of your eye
Just a touch away eternally
Waiting in the ethereal mist
She is the one who whispers
Our name when music inspires
Or a thing of great beauty
Captures our attention
And she is the one who embraces us
When we allow ourselves
The time to remember
Our own Soul

The Goddess

There I was in the ethereal mist
I was everything… And nothing all at once
And oh so long ago
I swam around your mind
As you finally dreamed me up
This idea of woman
You… you made me
Of stone and patch for your company
But you were lonely still
And so you took the wind
And filled me with it:
The Blessing of divine breath
Even so I stood as your creation
A thing of stone
What could bring your perfect beauty to life?

You mused over my sad perfection
And though you were the Master of all time
You could do little more than admire me

Alone for eons by the ethereal sea
Your stone goddess stood suspended in time
Unmoved by eternity
So perfect, so pristine
She never cracked a smile
Eons came and eons went
And with them storm and wrath
Your inner yearning
For the deep creation of humanity
Was more fervent than ever

For centuries beyond centuries,
I stood stone cold on the mountaintop
Until one day
My creator could no longer bear it
He took a chisel to my perfect form
And that was how it all began
From inside out the heat of the universe
Glowed through my heart
And warmed my flesh
It reddened my cheeks
It made me cry the tears of all time
And laugh for the greatness of God

My creator stood there before me and said,
"Human. Human woman that you be,
You were the toughest of all my creations
You plagued me through the eons
I wanted you of all my creatures
To be my perfect masterpiece
And then I knew the only way to give you life
Was to make you imperfect when all
Was said and done
And for this life your female heart will laugh
It will cry…. It will hate…It will learn
And it will love
And all this will fill the heart of the Universe
With a beauty that could only come from
The enigmatic nature of humanity
Now go into the night and live your life
I am very pleased".

The Bounty

Once again I return to the
Womb of Mother Earth
Where it is warm and deep
Where the silent melody lures
Me to a sacred sleep

We go here for the sweet inner dialogue
With the humors and the humus
With the seedlings and the sap
On the other side of the world

Where the cellos play their heart song
And the pentameter of eternity vibrates
Through the soil and the soul of the world

Waiting to give birth to the Newborn
And the Mother all at once

Now is the rich time for
The growing of all Souls
Ready for the harvest
And re geneses for all

Blessed Child

*O*pen your eyes young one

Blessed child
Not even Conscious of the world
You have been sleeping
In your mother's womb
For a long, long time
Open your eyes
And give a good cry
It won't be so hard

We were all innocent once
And came to learn about Humanity
And the lessons of the Soul
Some of us got distracted on the way
Or could not go beyond our ancestral woes

But you're ready for your awakening
And awareness of it all
To know thyself in every way
And Love the world as One

Mother

She is young
Mother is a creature of beauty
She stands tall above the reeds
As I look up to her
I am nearly blinded
By the golden rays of sunlight
That surround her
And I am convinced that she
Is some kind of eternal Goddess

It matters little that her mortal body was taken
When we were both young

Now I am old
But she remains
In time and space as she was
We spoke of infinite love long before
There was talk of death
Forever fixed within my heart
Is that image of my Goddess
Standing there amongst the field of dried grass
My little hand in hers

I imagine she would remember me as well
On our afternoon walk to the ocean
With the sun beating down on her little girl
And she thinking how remarkable life is
How fast the little ones grow
How they grow like weeds

Childhood is a precious time
But this image of mother and child
Is captured through eternity
The sun above my mother's hair like a halo
The sun shining down upon her daughter's

That moment in the field of reeds
Is as infinite as the soul of the world itself

We were there together, mother, daughter
And the eternal glow of the sun

Mothers and Sons

How does a Mother begin
To speak of her maternal love
Many of us would proclaim it from the hills
But we are silenced by its power
And can merely sit in wonder
As the little ones grow
Too big for our hold
And we have to let them go

We remember their first cry
When first they face the world
We remember their tenderness
That toughens through the years

We see our baby crawl then turn into the man
Remembering his very first breath
He remembering our last

I am the mother of a beautiful young man
I've gathered his childhood dreams
With the longings of his Soul
Wishing him safe harbor
On his long and winding road

I will love him his whole life long
And will wish the best for him
When I'm long gone
When he is the sage
The wise one …. The one
Who lives to tell his tales
And sing his songs
As Father to a son

The Mother will always be his Mother
Cradling that precious being
From the beginning to the end

We love our sons
We love our daughters
The greatest love of all
May our love be the tender
Their whole life long
And heal the world
They themselves bring with them
When all else seems to have fallen away

Even the mother

Gaia Speaks

How long ago was it
I seemed a different Woman
Barely recognizing myself
Once bitten by disease
The whole world seemed to change
Despite my respites and my love of life
And it was the very Nature
I adored and thrived upon
That altered my Life forever

Like some fierce undertow
That took me down and eroded my form
My perception of Life itself
Changed forever more

The wooded forests I played in as a child
Seemed to fail me in the end
They sent to me their toxic fairies
And poisoned nymphs thirsty for my blood

Why could they not have taken
The health of someone who cared less?
What happened to the innocent days
Of catching fireflies
In Midsummer Night Eves?

We have already destroyed this Earth
And I suppose we must pay the price
I was bitten long ago by the tiniest messenger
Of the Goddess Gaia, Mother Earth
And life as I knew it ended there

What did I know of Lyme's disease?
What does anyone know even today
Though I read somewhere
That the Seeds of Germ warfare
Fathered this disease

Doctors turn their backs on me over and over
And I realize
That we all turn our backs on the Earth
And we continue to murder
This extraordinary gift of God
Every day in every way
Her pain lives through me
Every time I have a relapse
As my total system breaks down
I realize how the Goddess cries through me
She cries for the peace and harmony
She felt before she lost control of her tides
She cries out in longing for the good health
She once knew before the pesticides came
And pollution swept the World

Now she lives in confusion and in chaos

She says
"I can no longer warn you of what's to come!
I am the living proof of the future
What will it take you to See
That the nature you destroy
Is the nature of which
You are an integral part
You dare to think
You stand separate from me?
You are naïve and arrogant all at once

Dear Ones,
I embrace you as I always have
And always will
I nurture you
And embrace you still
But I cannot help that my embrace
Has become pure poison
What did you expect?
Mankind, you were given
The gift of consciousness
Yet so many eons have come and gone
And you refuse to See what lies before your eyes

You are the guardians of the Planet
Do not fail me!"

The Original Wound

We all have an original wound...
Archetypal, Ancient,
Yet deeply personal
With a symbolic value
For each and every one of us

Perhaps such wounds are Sacred
And are meant to bring us closer
To the dilemmas of Humanity
In order to "work things out"

They are intricately woven into
The Tapestry of our lifetime
Connecting us to the very root of our destiny

It just may be that our Sacred Wounds
Are our greatest blessings
In the creation of our Journey
The creation of our Quest
Our hopes
Our dreams
Our awakenings
Our transformation
Our healing
Our evolution

Empress

I begin with mere essence
Of that which can be seen
Gazing upon beauty, I am stunned by
The levels of aliveness
In what I thought were mere objects
But now I look upon them
As if they are pieces of dreams
All that I have gathered in time
And oddly they look back at me
They silently tell me I am not alone
They tell me they are of the infinite ages
Beings of creation itself
And though they may not
Speak for themselves
They seek poets like me
To make deeper form and expression
Of their fine intent
I sit in the company of oh so many books
Sculptures of deities, of Gods, of Goddesses
Of Kuan yin, Buddha, Saraswati and Ganesh
Of paintings painted by others
And some by me
I sit with the gentle breeze
Conducting the dance of the reeds
Swaying sweetly before me
I sit with the spectrum of mornings' Light
In the presence of Spirit gazing back at me

They speak:

"Close your eyes Oh Human One
This is what we wish to say
You are not alone
The feeling of separation could dissolve
At any time when one's time is filled
With presence and with focus
Allow yourself to be touched Dear One
By the Spirit of everything
For here lies the Grace
You've been searching for
And the luminous Light
Of your wildest dreams
Here beyond the faintest veil
With the flutter
Of a thousand tiny
Angel wings
You are the Empress
And always were
Here to nurture the earth
To embrace with compassion
This whole wide World
And gather it up
With Love"

Picasso's Children

There is a great
Mythic melancholy
In the fields of time
Multi facets have
Come together
And split apart again
As each Self
Through Eons
Has felt the despair
Of that one loss

Perhaps we are all
Picasso's children
Made of oh so
Many fragments
Of time and space

Of many Mothers
Of many Fathers
Many Sisters
And many Brothers

Living in the Cosmos
As the Cosmos lives in us
Filling our Hearts
Filling our Souls

We are the lovers
Of the Universe
The Stardust
The Original
And the Final song

My Name

A rose by any other name May smell as sweet
But perhaps would not hold the same vibration
Or lead to the pathway of its original intent

Every time I think I have transcended, I am called back
"Erica...Erica" I am called by Mother.... "Erica"
I am called by another....
With a tone that contains the subtext,
"You are a bad girl, Erica, A very bad girl" .
"Erica," yells the next with his belt in hand
And finally, there comes the calling of my name
With the cunning lure to my childhood abuse

My name came to carry a weight despite its original intent
The name Erica was given to me by my mother
Who sought political freedom when she came to this country
"Am Erica" meant the land of the free
My name was meant to hold the key to
Individual, artistic, and spiritual freedom
But still holds the vibration of those
Who called my name with ill intent

A child wonders after a while, am I good or am I bad?
Am I worthless as they say? Lazy, spoiled, sullen, selfish?
Will I ever be free to feel what I feel?
Free to be the me I was meant to be?
Free from the addiction to a past ruled
By those who had been hurt themselves?

And now the Mother in me says to the child within,
"Erica, stand tall and free
Listen to the name called by Love
By the ones who call with affection, understanding, and respect

Hear your name as it was given
Hear it now and forever more
And be proud to go by the name, Erica
Old Soul of the highest order
The one who stands for Truth and Beauty
The one who stands for Spiritual Freedom
The one who stands for Peace
The one who stands on the Mountain high
Howling at the moon for the Mystic power of the Universe
The one who dares to dream the better dream
Erica do not forget who you are"

Beloved Rendezvous

Love Songs, Prayers, and
Conversations with the Beloved

The Heavenly Dreams

*P*erhaps a whisper called for us
Long before the World was born

Like the Suns, the Moons, and Stars above
Perhaps we came into our Being in response
To some beautiful thought

And one day, the sky opened wide
Sending forth seeds of Heavenly
Dreams upon the Earth
Each holding the secret code of Life
In all its glory
And all its Melancholy

Perhaps our Purpose came in first
Before the inkling of Mankind

And our Spirits were like birds in flight
Searching for their Home, their Destiny...

This may be the magnetism of our Lives
For a Soul seeks none other than its Reason
And actualization depends on it

Sometimes I think we are really here to fulfill
The Original Dream
Born of the Heavens above

Lighthouse

I live and I die
And I live again
And through the breakdown
Of my selfish little world
With all its fractures
Your Grace shines in…
I dreamt I lived in a cave
And couldn't find my way out…
A beam of Universal light
Came shining down on me from up above…
I was bathed in your love
And I shined like a star…
I held you in my heart…. for a while
But when I tried to take flight
Without you in sight
I fell from the sky
Like a bird with a wounded wing
And when I sailed the seas in the raging storm
Without your tower of guiding light
I got lost… I got lost…
You are my lighthouse
My compass and my shore
You are my truest anchor
When I am overcome by the scope of it all
But to serve you now I have to be strong
And so I will go to the Mountain if I have to
And I will go to the Temples if I must
I will heal and be healed
And I will get a hold of myself
For there is so much to do…

Beloved

Beloved
We meet once again my ancient friend
You who've touched me with your Ocean Breeze
And the waves that kiss the shore
You have warmed me
Through the Eons in Sunglow
And cradled my Soul
In the eternal shadow of the night
But today I saw you
In a stranger's eye
As we encountered each other
Like sisters from another Land
Her name was Isabella
Even the name was familiar
But Life itself is familiar these days
For I recognize You in everything
I thought I glimpsed You, Beloved
Long ago and far away
But it was always You
In the here and now
And it was always You
In the lives of every Man and Woman
From here to Eternity
In the eye of the Stranger
Lives the Sacred
Humankind You are my old friend
And I am Yours!

Gratitude

I woke earlier than usual this morning yet
Remained in half twilight for a while
Knowing this day was about gratitude
I pondered all that I could be thankful for at
This time of flux in the world

In many ways we turn in on ourselves
And turn so many away

And then it all came rushing in
All that I am thankful for
And that is everything!

And all it took was opening these eyes to see

May I hold this "seeing"
When I sit with friends today
And may I recall this "seeing"
Through many tomorrows
I am grateful for you
I am grateful for me
I am grateful for my husband
For my son
For all my friends
To loved ones present and loved ones lost
Though never lost to me

I am grateful for my childhood
Now held in memory
Of Mother, Father, Sister, Brother
To all my family

For those I have known, or tried to know
And those I've tried to Love
And best of all, to the Universe above
Who lives within us all

Forever Young

I speak to you now in silence
Oh Great One ...Beloved of Mine
I meditate upon an inner vision of you
Or should I say
An inner feeling

Your mystique has held your
Secret lo these many years
Like a brilliant lure
That I may forever seek you
Draw you, Dance you
That I may forever write your Poem

You are the masterful artist
There is no other

One day I woke to your love
And nothing else mattered
And yet because you are everything
Everything matters

Let me sing your song, the Song of Songs
Let me color the world with your breath
Let me dance your eternal dance

As old as the Ages as I am
Through you, I am forever young

Cosmic Lover

Dear One,
We made a pact you and I
And I hold you to it

We agreed there would be joy
There would be sorrow
There would be wounding

We agreed that through this life
You would take the risk for all or nothing
This contract was not made on the fly
Nor did we agree to a shallow life
Of creature comfort

You have a job to do
Woman of the multi cosmos
Standing now for all
Who would listen through you

You are Don Juan,
Lover of the one and the many
Wearer of a thousand faces of eternity

You agreed to meet at the crossroads where
Consciousness and unconsciousness
Come together
Where God and devil have it out

Stay with verve and bring forth
Your passion for your evolving mission
Bring forth your voice and heart

Stand tall and true with fierce love
Where the North Star shines upon the earth

Be the cosmic alchemist
Spin the eternal spiral
At the cross point of divine source
For you are a master coming into your own
And you have brought
The Mystical, Magical gifts
Ripened and ready
For the holographic cause
Spread them far and wide
And through the dimensions
Cosmic lover that you are

The Final Dance

I wake early just to be with you Beloved
Ours is an eternal love affair
With lapses between our rendezvous
You beloved life
You've been generous, so generous
To welcome me back time and again
I must seem like a fickle lover
Coming and going like the changing winds
But you always stand by me don't you

Forgive me, I am but a foolish wanderer
Adventuring off when whims take me
Some of us have restless hearts and the truth is
I am old and tire out quickly these days
I am not as resilient as I used to be
And so often feel like Amelia lost at sea
Perhaps once you reach a certain age you
Ought not to fly so far

But You know I have always
Found my way back to you
Just when I thought I had forgotten my reason
And my purpose for going on

You would come to me in the night
And call my name

You would say,
"Goddess of mine,
You are younger than you think
Gather yourself and begin again
And take my hand, my Love

The final dance is ours, Dear One
For endless time
And endless Love"

The House of Gathering

You insist on waiting
At the very bottom of this vessel…
Down in the depths
Till I have finished with my fancies…
And am back in the fields
Of absolute Nothingness
And there at once
You flicker your eternal flame
And ignite me
I am in the House of Gathering
After the death of the Self I once knew
I am gathering my bones, my blood,
And the pieces of my Heart
Even so, the mirror's reflection
Is not of the one I once knew
Who stares back at me but You
Or perhaps the Me I was meant to be
And as for your flickering illumination
That is the one thing I remember from long ago
When the memory of facts has nearly vanished
I saw your light in sheer delight
Chasing fireflies one night
When tragedy was replaced
By magical thinking
I saw your light by the silvery moon
Each "tuck in time"
With one I loved and lost too soon
And oh so long ago
I saw your Light illuminate through me
On Sacred Stages and Sacred pages

And there have been times
Of such great yearning moving through me
So filled with a Mythic passion
That I can only assume
It was The Chi of the World itself
Answering the call To Cosmic Love
And Cosmic yearning
Yes, that's it!
It was the yearning of the Cosmic Seed
Waiting to burst through me... through me!
Through this little Ego shell...
So thick with Human illusion
Yet willing enough to embrace
The will of the Great Life Force
And to accept my fate and destiny
For this is the Doctrine of my Life:
To be the container of something greater
To be the flute for the God Song
To be the Mind through which that Greater
Might "think" on itself
To be the eye that finally
Through many lifetimes in one
(With white hair upon my head)
Sees not the projections of Human psychology
But the Truth of our Human condition
And the Vision of our Human Evolution

So, this is it...
I am living in my Evolving Mission
So, tell me Life,
Now that you've filled my days
With all your Passion
Why now do I feel so old... so quiet... so still?
Yes, why do these later years
Bring me to this place
Of near emptiness just when I have embraced
All that is authentic
And ripened for the World Work?
Are you there Beloved,
Resting in the cave that once held my life?
Are we done with drive and effort?
Are we done trying to make a difference?

The Beloved speaks:
"You are in the House of Gathering
And you needed space
To Gather the best of your life
The best of your history... the best of all things
Gather the highest and gather wisely
Gather yourself in your arms
Like a Great Mother ready to hold the World
Gather in quiet ritual
What is now needed for these times

For this great venture…
This adventure, one must be properly prepared
No baggage please… No junk DNA
No illusions, no confusions
No regret, blame, or guilt
No judgment, no jealousy
No holding heavy burdens
Or false assumptions
No recriminations
No controls

But most of all
No self-loathing
No No No
Yes, You are in the House of Gathering
Ready for re-genesis… ready for re-birth
And in the emptiness waiting to be filled
With all your Gatherings
Start with this:
Deep Love….Deep compassion…
Deep clarity…..Deep soul
Deep inspiration
Deep wisdom of the multi ages
Deep generosity of your intimate self
Deep flexibility in relationship to the World
And to conflicts large and small

Deep holding of Higher Vision
And deep co-creating in the ever
Expanding evolution of the One and the Many
Now, we begin again,
Perhaps like the Eternal Pendulum
Swinging through eons, through centuries,
Through "infinite oscillations
Repeating the Epochs of time"
Once more and once more and once more
In this… Divine dance of Eternity
Just this time with the Awakening
And Quickening for All
And with a quiet Grace you have never known
And the courage of a thousand Heroes who made
Their way across the waves
Quiet now, quiet now
There there
This is the beginning
Once more"

Arms Wide Open in The House of Longing

For Eons

Do all artists suffer
In yearning for transformation?
Does the flower suffer?
Does the ocean?
Does the moon disappear at dawn
Ashamed that she hasn't sung
Her greatest song?
Does she feel belittled because too few
Acknowledged her in her shining hour?

Everyone slept through the evening show
And forgot her in the morning
Yet like me she keeps trying

She has come every night for eons
She comes to sing her song

I Am a Miner

You will not see me frolicking
In the Town Square
Done up for your amusement and good cheer
I have turned in my dancing shoes
And rosy cheeks
In favor of my solitude

I'm going down for the season
To where the night crawler lives
Where the golden roots
Of my Mythic life all began

This is the work of my soul:
To burrow deep down where treasures lie

I can't help myself
I must be a changeling with
A hunger to be in and of this World
In its highest…In its widest…
In its lowest…In its deepest sense…

I like to get these hands dirty, yes
To unearth the unseen
And get into the grit of Life
Of mine and even yours

I am a miner for that Holy Grail
That lives within us all
Digging beneath the illusions
Designed by this civilized world

I am a miner for a Human Heart
The treasure of all worth
Digging down for my Golden bones
In the deep rooted Soul of the Earth

Ohas Dancing

You don't have to travel to the
Deep jungles of South America
To know the way of the Shaman
Though such journeys may rekindle
The memory of long ago…
The Soul is Eternal
We've been there before

The Soul knows the path
Of the great Medicine Man
He is the one who knows the Dance of the Fire
And holds the Vision of the ages
Through time Future, present and past
There are messages left on the wind

There are those of us who have lived
The Shaman's life
We remember only vaguely
Through our psychic sense of things
And the metaphors of our Mythic tales

Lifetimes spill into the next
And an old drum beat
Resounds with the setting of the sun
Your Vision Quest is the very life you've lived

The Angel of Death embraced you at birth
And she said,

"I will be with you always...
I am your loving Usher...
I'll guide your breath and teach you
The way through Karma and such...
I'll teach you the way of your Nature
And the Nature of all things...

Feel your Life! Feel it! Dance
The Dance of the Ancient Ohas!

And know that everything you ever
Thought was the work of the Devil
Was the work of God Himself!"

The Artist

Do what you must to work out your lives
So that the bliss, the mission, the love
Come first
Then create beauty out of horror
Create love out of hate
Take ugliness and chisel it down
Till the gem is revealed
Transform… Transmute
Spin the elements well
For the enlivening of
The elemental force
Of the greater good
Be the alchemist
Work this crucible in
Need of creativity
Take on the challenge
Of this topsy-turvy world
And do it like an artist
We are working on evolution you and I
We are working on expansion
We are working on human potential
We are working on Unity
You say you are an artist
Well then, paint the World
Sing the World
Dance the World
Play the World
Write the World
And right the World!

Yearning

You tell me there is a yearning
Within you that will not seize
Yet when I ask you to speak of it
You bow your head
With a certain vulnerability
And peculiar judgment of yourself
As if to say, to want of anything is Fool's play
As if to need is negative and less than heroic
Such yearning exposes a Human Being
As being Human
And so you hide your yearning
Along with your wounds
And alas… your Light
But in the day of the quickening I ask you
To gather your desire in your own two hands
And listen to the words I say
It is the yearning of the seed
To burst through the Earth
That she may be free to grow
It is the yearning of the Pearl to break the shell
And the yearning of the dove to shatter the egg
That she might one day take the flight
That is her Birthright
Take your yearning
And bust through the ego shell
Bust through with a passion and vengeance
That you might one day be free
Grow wings and fly
Grow conscious… grow love…grow soul
Grow Human…Grow!

My Soul's Prayer

What is your heart's desire, you who live
Among others with longing in their souls?

My desire:
To live in liberation of small thought
And small concerns
To encounter the dawn each day
And to see the world
In all its glory

To listen to my soul
Whose only want
Is to do Good in the world
And make manifest its essence
From hill and dale

To empower my fellow man
With all I have received
And all I have learned
Whether from experience
From mentors
Or from the Gods above

To give....
To be the gift and the given

To teach, to inspire, to nurture
To make beauty

To divine…
To divine through song
Through prose, through story
Through art, through dance
Through my particular role
In the new genesis

To bring the Sacred into the mundane
To lift, to dig, to shed light, to love
To take the all that I am
On the road to Kingdom Come
To help the world come together
In Divine integration

And to hold the ego of the world
With compassion
While holding space for You
Oh Great One
Oh Great Mother
Oh Divine One
Oh Sacred Love

Passion

This is what comes to me
This is what wants to come through me
This is the river flow
This is the blood of ages
This is the color red
This is my wounded heart
This is my joy, my energy, my inner chi
My electricity, my motivation
My bliss, my rich Soul
My rich history, my culture
My ancestry

Passion!
This is the stuff of all life
The howl of the wolf
The gypsy's tango
Passion!
This is my inner youth still full of dreams
Still living in its bliss
Passion!
This is my heartfelt prayer for a world at peace
And passionate about its passion
The passion of humanity against all odds
Passion... the color red
The fire inside the belly
The fervent expression
Of the best of who we are
And who we were meant to be
Passion!

Get Soul

I wish for the highest
For a string theory
That holds us in a loving embrace
Not just for the intellectual or the scientific
But for the future of humanity
What will it take to be fully human
And at our best?

Evolution cannot truly be achieved
Through mere transcendence
And this virtual world is proof enough that
Something Sacred has been lost
Children are killing children
And there are no promises
That all will end well
The alchemical crucible is spinning fast
But what will rise to the top
Without the key ingredient
We seem to have lost

What is needed now more than ever before
Comes from the Center of it all
The glue that binds
The stuff of love

Good God Mankind, hold each other
Commune …Connect….Get Soul
Get God!

Hunger

I hunger for justice
I hunger for love
I hunger for the kind
Of compassion that fulfills
Because the connection is true
Because the connection is deep
And born of receptivity

I hunger for philosophy
I hunger for the kind of
Give and take that you
Can imagine of the old Greeks
I long to share Soul to Soul
To sit with the greatness of you
And the greatness of me

I hunger for the Soul of man
And the soul of the world

I long for co-creation, the only thing
That will fill this existential loneliness
I hunger to be understood
I hunger for travel and when
I do not get enough of it
I either travel the Sacred road
Or indeed I spin wheels

I hunger for beauty
I long for the highest
I long to work out this thing
Called Life for you and for me

I hunger for all of this
Yet struggle to this day with
The paradox of being an introvert
Who hungers for company

Maybe it's because what I truly hunger for
Is the God that lives in you
And the God that lives in me

Without You

If you could gather all that you wished for
Your arms would hold the World
And extend to Galaxies unknown to Man
Gathering the rivers and the seas
The living waters of the World

Your thirst could only be quenched
By many lifetimes
For one could simply never do

Nothing could satiate
Your Heart and Soul
But Infinity itself
Do not feel ashamed
To want of Love
Is your Birthright
While sharing yourself
With the World

To want to see and to be seen
Is not only the necessity of one's Soul
But is a key to World Peace

To want to create something
Greater than what came before
Is exactly what we ask of Humanity
A creative urge so great
That against all odds
The Earth can continue to revolve

These are the wants
Of the Universe itself
Finding their way
Through your Heart

We've come to you
Dear Humanity
Because you dare
To carry the passion
And need of ours
To grow the World!
The Human seed
Was planted long ago
With the dream
Of the Gods themselves
And the plan was for
The expansion
Of Infinity itself

Without the Passion
You were born to feel
Nothing would get done

 Dreams

*O*nce you begin to dream
That dreaming can instantaneously
Lift your frequency

Dreaming opens the possibility
For the muse to return
Dreaming can usher the thousand and one
Tiny angels through the veil
All of whom prepare for the dream's gifting

Every blessed entity
Goes to work on your behalf
Opening the portal to the great wide open
Where all things are possible

The beginning of such dreaming
Comes with grace, with joy
And with ecstasy
One must allow
The fertile dream
To have its life
Allow no worries to interfere
Allow no doubt to intercept
The magic of the night

Your imagination
May merely have let the messenger in
And if you fail to manifest the dream yourself
Someone else surely will

Dear ones
We all have to give our gifts away
One way or another
So think your lovely thoughts
And rejoice that the dream
Has landed somewhere

Dream your dreams
Worthy of greatness
They may have
More power than
You think

Mythic Voyages in the Tides of Change

Embracing Fate and Destiny

Mandala

$\mathcal{J}$ saw the image of a three dimensional
Mandala in my dream the other night
I picked up the Center of the great spiral
And pulled it out of itself
Until it was straight and taught
I then saw how it could touch the
World at any place it chose

Stretched to its fullest, it looked like a snake!
A snake with an Angelic face and a mouth
That wanted to kiss the World

Pulled from its Center, I saw it as
The Chord of Truth and Power
Its presence was awe-inspiring
And I felt blessed to have witnessed
Such a Sacred Image

Never will I let the Demon on my Path rip
This Elegance from my Memory
It carries the Soul of the Ancient Traveler
Who journeys through simultaneous time
Into the Cosmos!

Beyond Eternity

There has been a calling
From the heavens
From way beyond eternity
Once there was a vast
And Mythic emptiness
Yet the eternal prayer
Began like a silent song
The call has culled
The One and the Many
The "Everyman"
From "every land"
From "every time"
Known to Man
Has spun in circles
At God's hand
Spinning upwards
In transcendence and joy
Spinning downwards
To the depths
Of ancient sorrow
Some of us have cried
The tears of Humanity
But are here
To answer
The Call

Ancient Heroine

I am the Narrator of my own tale,
Though I have been on many stages
And have worn many masks
It is an ancient tale that has unfolded
Through the Eons
As I Dance before old Gods and New
We grow from our experiences
Each and every one of us...
And in so doing participate in the expansion
Of this Great Eternal Land

Infinity seems to feed on all our passions...
As we reverberate into far away regions
How can we be so young and yet so old?
Is it because we are of time and timelessness?
We are Body and we are Soul
We are the stuff of Eternity
And therefore Eternal

We are the Ancient travelers
On the road to kingdom come
With the tale of the One and the Many
And the Dreams of the Many and the One

Land of Lot

I have been traveling through the Land of Lot
Remembering my gypsy tune
I've held lifetimes of many
And many did I love
I've seen the everlasting reflections
Of my ancestors
And they cry their tears through me
I am haunted by their stories
Like an empath open to eternity's sorrows
I am haunted by holocausts
And by those who could not bear
The long road to freedom

Some threw themselves off the large ships
Fleeing from the Nazis, fleeing from their lives
Always sailing the rough seas
To get to the other side
The trip is familiar in some Mythic sense
The fog is thick, so thick that if one got lost
Others would not know for some time

I heard the story of a long lost Aunt
Who committed suicide
On the last ship to come to America
During the Nazi invasion
Did she not want the freedom
That was promised?
Could she not bear life's tragedies
Or trust it could ever get better?

Had she lost loved ones
In gas chambers and simply
Could not go on without them?
Did she carry the everlasting family miasma
Handed down over centuries
That sadly affects us all?

We gypsies wander restlessly
We play the tune of ages past and ages present
We read the future for we feel
With passionate hearts in this human land
We dance for the soul of our lost ones
The ones who could not accept their lot

There is a destiny for us all
Sometimes it can only be found
At the end of the road
When one is done with his gypsy wanderings
When he walks the earth
With all the Ancestors far and wide
And returns to the place he came from
Where the deep sea meets
The tallest mountain
And the clouds hang low
Like a coverlet for the Soul
Where the fog is so thick, one could get lost
And never be seen or heard from again
But alas one has come home

There is a place somewhere in France
It goes by the name Lot
It has a truly mystical atmosphere about it
Like a land forgotten but always welcoming
To gypsy hearts like mine

Perhaps we are all wanderers
In search of a final destiny
Not knowing it may lie
In misty Lands like Lot

If you listen carefully
You can hear the far-off melody
Of a thousand violins
I hope with all my heart
That my sad, lost aunt
Who jumped ship one night at sea
Is with fiddle in hand
Playing as only gypsies can
The song of World Peace

The Lonely Journey

I wish to speak the truth of my Soul
But only the hills know of my story
Pieces of this life
Are now scattered
On the wind

I am the ocean
I am the emerald forest
I am split open as shattered
Fragments land here
There and everywhere
Yet seemingly nowhere anymore

We are nothing
Without another to receive us

Destiny Finds Us

Destiny finds you when you least expect it
And often in your darkest hour
It enters just when fate has backed
You against the wall
Your only hope is for some attempt to rescue
Your Soul from your ill-fated lot
But the fact is you may be witnessing
The Divine Partnership of shadow and light
And you are merely being escorted
Towards your very own calling

Sometimes it has to get bad.. really bad
Before we take full responsibility for our lives
The fates seem to break into our
Falsehoods and fancies
Like dark angels in the night that say

"Surrender now...
Go to the depths of your being...
To the urge behind your Purpose
Into the power of your Destiny
You are the workers of the world
Some of you carry a lightness of being
Some of you carry a heavy load
In one way or the other, you are here to help
The World spin round while weaving
The tales of Yore

You are an eternal hero with much to tell
So tell it well you Hamlet, you Eros, you Psyche, you Soul

You have an ancient heritage
To worlds held secret to most
Tell the story you came to tell
And remember what you stood for
All the time you lived and died
And now live again once more

You are the crier
For the Soul of the World!
You who stand for something!

Are you the maker of poetry?
Are you the maker of art?
Are you the maker of new form and thought
With a deeply passionate Heart?
Are you healer, teacher, philosopher?
Do you stand for a thousand souls?
Are you here for justice?
Are you here for Truth?
Are you here to change the world?

The Eons have waited on you my friend
Waited to hear your Word"

L' Destiny

L' Destiny is here in this very moment
Though this moment is filled
With the depth and breadth
Of one's history and one's future

The ancient fields fill life
With the soul of the ages
They fill one's life with life

Destiny is here in the moment
Yet beckoned by the whispering pines
And ushered to the portal
Of limitless possibility

My destiny is passion filled
It is not some mere acquisition or career

Perhaps we live our destiny
At any given time
But any given time exists
At Ground Zero
Where Cosmic Fools
Can spiral round and round
For an Eternity

I have found my destination
After traveling the eons

Though there is nothing final about it

My destiny contains vitality despite
The so-called arrival one assumes

It is the dance of the shape-shifting Soul
Centered at a Sacred Fulcrum
Growing lighter
And Brighter
And more exquisite
Every day

Taking the Leap

I stood on the edge of my Life
And looked out over the Horizon
I trembled at the thought
Of leaping to the other side
For fear of the unknown
I knew I needed the help
Of the Universe
For if I were to have fallen
Through the chasm
The angels might catch me
And lift me once again

It is many years later
And I stand on the other side
Wondering what took me
So long to get here
And why I hadn't known
That the leap
Was just one small step
But I must have been lost
In the shadows of sorrow
Of grief... and the despair of the past

Now I have landed on a new World
In a terrain blossoming bright
I am here thanks to you, Beloved
And to my Ancient Soul who yearned
To be a part of these changing times
In the Land of Constant Genesis

The Horizon beckons me to look
Towards the future with hope
And simultaneously remember
The first inkling of my own Soul's purpose

The Future does not have to be forced
Perhaps it is already here announcing itself
Through one's future self
One's True Self…. One's Divine Self
Who waits for you with open arms
The very One who calls your name
In the Eternal Night
In your Dreams
Your hopes
Your yearning
Your bliss

In your Sacred Wounds
And in your existential loneliness

Listen to the call of your Own…

Embracing the Paradox

The universe has handed us
Its beautiful mystery
A paradox for all Time
That we might use our mind
That we might co-create
A new and better template for
Ourselves and for the giver of the gift

Puzzles should stimulate
And this one was not meant for unwise fools
The mystery says: "Figure it out
You are a thousand layers deep
Of timelessness of ages past
Of present and of future

You are the cells of one another
Multiplied a trillion times
Broken up and broken down

You are the pieces of eternity's dream
Here to grab hold of your place

Life is but a Mystery
The lure of your Soul
Inherent in your fate
Inherent in your call!"

Sea of Change

These are the times of magnetic extremes
And the soul of man is struggling to find
Some semblance of meaning
Beyond the stories told

Be still, my Love
Take this Cosmic Love
And wrap yourselves well
And know that at this time
Of converging energies
Truth will seem like a disappearing act:
Now you know with Gnostic knowing
Now you do not

Perhaps this is the very process
Of Alchemy itself
And the World pot is spinning
Beyond your control

Stay with Love, oh, stay with Faith
For you are paddling in the Sea of Change
This is the story... There is no other
So lend your hand and heart
To you brother

Hope Springs

Walk with beauty, the Navajos say
While the Hopis warn of the times to come
In truth, the future arrived long ago
Casting its shadow before us
There is a word for their prediction:
"Koyaniskatsi" It means... World out of balance
Even the Earth knows what we have done
To the nature of things
And natural order seems to be no more
You wonder why the floods have come
They are the tears of the Mother
Grieving the loss of harmony
And naturally she responds
With natural disaster
Over and over and over again
We, the beings of this planet
Have gone out of control
Living our lives through extremes
Living in the throes of extreme conflict
Extreme chaos, extreme confusion
And extreme despair
It would seem we have gone completely mad
And will soon be running wild in the streets
Perhaps the Hopis knew well
Of what some might call "The End Days"
And yet, there is a strange and ever mysterious
Cosmic law that brings hope against the odds

Hope springs in the worst of times
With an urge within every living thing
To seek balance even when order is no more
The tree of Life may need
A good cry now and then
But she stands tall and majestic
Despite her woes
Her roots are too deep and ancient
To give up just because
Of the foolishness of mankind
Her limbs reach out to all of us
With an eternal compassion
We must look to her now
With compassion in return
We must learn from her now
The secret of nurturing
In the face of the toughest of times
Hold your heads high, she says
And dig deep into your ancient roots
For your reserve, your resolve, your resources,
Your greater wisdom, your eternal love
We can get through this
We can build a new garden for the times
Walk with beauty she says
Walk with hope.... Walk with Faith
Walk with understanding...Walk with Grace
Walk with the knowing that all will be well
For we have the will of The Universe in us all

Against the Odds

Despite mood, sickness, abuse
Despite loss, grief, insanity
Despite the Devil himself
We must gather our compassion for all that is
Within our own two hands
And cup Humanity with Radical Love

I have tried... and so have you
But Radical Love does not come easily
When the veils have fallen away
And what remains is a constant casting
Of Human shadow…
And an old paradigm
Snapping at the heels
Of the new one in waiting
Gasping for its final breath

There are dragon hearts beneath the surface
And with a great unearthing
They're spewing fire through the innocent...
Even the children have gone mad

But we were warned of these times
And though we may not be
In the throes of another World War
All energies are in collision
And the World itself is on the brink

One day it might finally break
Break down, break apart, break open
They say destruction is needed
Before the new dawn
That demolition
Of what has not worked is inevitable
For the building of the stronger foundation
Evolution is in the air
And the Mystery will do its work
Beyond our conscious awareness

But we are being asked
For something more
We are being asked to bring
Our Souls to the cause
And not for the fancies of the Gods

It is up to us to mend the World
And make it whole with Love

Why Not?

Last night I woke with a terrible fright to an electrical storm unlike anything I have ever witnessed. It was so intense I imagined within my fear-filled mind the wildest of thoughts. My eyes aching from the brightness of the light. It was truly terrifying and at a somewhat terrifying time on this planet. The world has certainly been at odds with itself. The weather systems have gone haywire. We are in the throes of Global warming. And in the throes of conflict in most every way. Why would a nuclear event be so very farfetched? History has told enough disaster tales to assume I was simply being foolish. We were all afraid… and I am certain the whole neighborhood stood by their windows holding on to their own.

Hours later the storm finally subsided and with it most of our anxiety. But before retiring, I said a little prayer still wondering what we would find in the morning. What would we learn of this most terrible night? Drama and doom, once they enter your House, are not easy to extinguish.

Life is known to turn on a dime however… and somehow in the dead of night, all signs of the demonic display had vanished. And in the morning when I woke, I felt the tenderest embrace of light beams casting through my window warming me with a most remarkable sense of calm and beauty. It felt like the Beloved was smiling from within filling me with the truth of Life's absolute perfection. And I had to laugh at myself and the melodrama I'd experienced only hours before.

And then I thought a most curious thought. Perhaps last night, I had actually "seen the Light." Yes, perhaps I had seen the Light... Surely, that light could have meant any number of terrible things, but it was still the light of the World. And today I realized I had seen something Sacred. Only fear had blotted it out.

What if we truly understood that the Light of the world is always present?... What if we always felt its love? Imagine if we could always feel love of self and love of others without judgment beyond the judgment that all is well? Would that we could feel this always. Would that we could transcend our fears.

Life is an abstraction... And as such, lends itself to all sorts of conclusions. Our minds are wild... With wild imaginations incessantly thinking up narratives of all creation because in fact, we are creative...So with the power to create why not create beauty? Why not create love? Why not create a World that works?

And a beacon of Light for safe harbor to all!

The Eternal Flame

I was born with a certain miasma
Apparently etched into my soul
I might have known I would
Suffer loss over and over
Eventually we all must learn
To let go of everything
And perhaps if we are born
With a spiritual hunger
We will learn more quickly
Than most to let go and let God

When I was very little
I already knew what it was like
To be left alone
To know of abandonment
Such feelings, such experiences
Will burn your heart and Soul
And you walk with their shackles
Your livelong days

To get through the labyrinth of your life
To the very center of it all
You must navigate well
Through All the complexes
That you set up long ago

En route you will find the symbols and
The impressions of every moment lived
The so-called bad times were
Every bit as important as the good

Give thanks within the walls of your labyrinth
I have heard tell of walls melting away at once
Where gratitude was felt
It would seem challenging
To thank all those who hurt you
Who abandoned you
Who rejected you
Left you on your own

But thank them all I do

Softening

One's challenges change in tone
And meaning over the years
And hopefully there is a softening of ego
So that shadows can be faced head-on
So that one's highest potential can
Reside harmoniously with one's Soul
And one's more mature local self

Yes, the ego must soften
As the earth softens enough to let nutrients
Bring forth the flower from the seed
We must allow for the opening of all that is good
And it takes a softening

It takes a softening and an inner nurturing
It takes a form of listening for
The guidance of the highest

Our complexes are right next to
The diamond of our innermost Self
The Self that wants to fly freely on angel wings
What lies beneath the surface
Of our complexes can serve
But they must be dismantled gently
And the all that we are
Must begin again many times over
If we are to get it right

We must learn the right use of will
The right use of power...
The right use of conflict
Of our strengths
Our weaknesses...
Our passions
Our intellect....
Our talents
Our minds....
Our energies
Our dreams....
Our calling

We all have a journey
May we help each other evolve
May we take each other on
And if we cannot
May we at least give
Our truest blessing

May we have a softening

World Wounding

Understand that world wounding
May be as essential as personal wounding
And that these divine tragedies
Occurring at this time are not to be forgotten
On the Sacred level there is purpose
And it just may be to break the World Heart open
For higher and greater compassion for itself

This is the Sacred Stage
And you are being nudged
To hold the bigger picture
Now and forever more

Yes, you have separated yourselves
From each other with your own stories…
But still can't seem to grasp
The fact that you yourselves
Have chosen to step into
Each other's projections
To play out your lives

Dear Ones,
It is time to look
Through the lens
Of Unity consciousness
It is time the Cosmic Seed
Within each one of you
Gives birth to the greater
More loving you waiting to be born

You are being asked now
To drop illusions
Drop confusions

Your very Soul and Higher Self
Are in embrace
And together are embraced
By the Soul of Eternity

And in the Quantum Field
All is embraced by that Love
Every Human that has ever lived
Every planet, every star,
Every multi self
In its infinite dimensions

Yes… Every sun, every moon
Every grain of sand
Every snowflake
Every being

Through Infinity
And back again

Embracing Eternity

Gathering Wisdom in the Remaining Years

Hallelujah

Why do we lose ourselves
When we grow old?
Perhaps it is the losing
Of what was that drives
Our soul more fervently
Towards you Beloved
Perhaps it is in our loss
That we reach for the chalice
And sometimes quench that
Great thirst with
A great Hallelujah

My Mortality

All is reflected
In the mirror of another
In their eyes, their words
And even on the wind
Life is a living symbol
A connected field of goings on
Reflected in the outer world
They say the inner world needs
An outer drama to live in
It is the mythic way of the Soul
Our lives are not random
And even the projections
Of another's shadow upon us
Is somehow interwoven
With our dramatic narrative
A narrative as old as time

These are my later days
And I am grappling with the inevitable
As if the Universal dilemma of all time
Is trying to work itself out through me
As I question my mortality
The ultimate Fate has come to pass
In the divine drama of life and death
As their forces go into battle within me

I no longer live
For what I am to become
Or what I am to make of myself
That forward movement
Of my life's purpose
Has changed in tone and velocity
For the force of what has to come
Resists my life

All we ever wanted
In the "marketplace"
Was a kind of immortality
And though the Soul of a man
Is as vast as the Infinite
It cannot be held in one's grasp
Despite its deep and true substance

Still, it secretly holds
What it is we are after
In the face of growing old

Live today from the inside out
There you will find eternity

Old Folks

Memories fade
Older ages like to
Wipe the slate clean I suppose
Wisdom says,
It's time for me
To take the center stage
You had your turn in the spotlight
While flirting with the World
One's purpose can expand after a time
It does not have to diminish
As our bodies wither with the sands of time

Yes, we have become the old folks
We once ignored and put to pasture
Thinking life was meant for youth

But I am all ages in one
And the truth of this matter is such:
I have been forced by gravity to sit in this place
Like the Empress spinning silk

I wait for you with open arms
Please take a little time on
The road to your kingdom come
For a visit now and then

We Elders have treasures to share
Beyond your imaginings
And we need you to receive our wise offerings
Less you diminish what we have come here for

Human life requires a giving and receiving
And a giving back again
Young ones seem almost too busy
For such interplay
But we have no choice in the matter
But to thrive on our usefulness

My arms are open wide
Pray, fall into me

Winter Days

You've grown your Soul through Winter Days
And now you'd like to rest, you say

It's true… One mustn't waste Divine energy
Or force its diminishment
Through Will's ineptitudes

Be still… Be quiet…
No judgment… No remorse…
You've lost your youth, your talent, your chi
Your genius, your Muse, your Memory

They will not offer you their hand
But smile upon your Human dilemma
For the Spirits of life have an uncanny
Way of keeping the Soul intact

The best of being never dies
It lives on through Infinity…

Passion does not care about
Your lack of youthful tone
Genius does not care about your memory
Beauty does not care about your fading looks
For Life wants in, no matter how you feel

Dear One, we all know the law of the land
When it comes to growing old

Remember the law of your Soul and the
One who was made immortal a long time ago

You were the one who partnered
With Eros Himself
To create in the World
The greatest joy
Of all time

Spirit will always find a way to inspire
Even through the Winter Days

The Piper is just a step away
For the sake of your eternal Song

Woman in the Mirror

These written pages are stained with red
The blood of my ego's death
The tears of my life…

Sometimes I feel like an ancient Shaman
Standing on the hill without grounding
And oh how I have been struck by lightning
So many times that by now I should
Be humbled by the Truth of Ages
Determined to get through to me

What was it I would not see?
I thought I stood for Truth
With little left to learn
I have been to the Mountain
And have died a thousand deaths
What more do I need to be
The best of what I was meant to be

These past months while I lay low
I watched over my body and Soul
No one came to my Funeral… but me
I stood by as observer and deceased
The mourner and the mourned

Laying in the casket stillness
Washed over the World

There was nothing at all
To concern myself with
No judgment… no tension
No want, no purpose
No pain.. no joy.. no breath

And who were the pallbearers
At the procession?
Who were the many
Who stood in solemn prayer?

I am no longer certain of anything
But I think they were me
They were all me

And like a miracle
I rose above my sarcophagus
Ready to return to the light of day
Renewed, reborn and ready to serve
Ready for my Holy Work
For those who would receive me
And now I see what I never could see
My part in all this mess

I am the Woman in the Mirror
Goddess and Devil at once

Gathering the One

It's hard to reveal our innermost secrets
Though we sit and talk philosophy
I speak of my longings....
You speak of your woes
But still we do not know each other
We know little of the aching heart
Of our fellow man
And we seem to have little room for the truth
Behind the relationship's mask

Who is intimate these days?
I myself feel less alone in my aloneness
For souls, meet souls in silence
Oh sweet silence
Sweet field of faith
Sweet ancient land of mythos
Sweet essence
Sweet me

People still fear each other
They don't like that which is Unique
And though the new paradigm
Yearns to fulfill the dream of Unity
There remains that ever-constant
Remnant within the Human psyche
Called prejudice
And it stands against
The very thing we are going for
Radical love....Radical compassion

We are Divine and indeed we are One
But as long as men judge others we fail
At our own ambition to act as One

I am from that generation
That lived for "love and peace"
We lived for the freedom of speech
And the freedom to be exactly
Who we were designed to be

We honored each other for that
And encouraged each other to speak our Truth
There is a voice within us
And our souls have a longing to express
But we are judged harshly for having beliefs
That may not match up to each other

We may not string each other up for
Our different skin color anymore
Or burn each other at the stake
But for pity's sake
What will it take
To finally gather
The One

House of Mirrors

I loved you my fellow man,
My friend, my foe, my husband
My sister, my father, my mother
I loved you everyman
I loved you but I was wounded
In that space between your words
Which silently said: "But I don't love you
And since I loathe myself as I do
I am stuck with loathing you too"

And so with my open, vulnerable heart
I am struck at the center of my being
From the fear and judgment
That we all seem to possess

God is there in the beginning of love
But the spirits of Psyche and Eros
Get spooked easily
Why did we dare to enter
The House of Mirrors in the first place?

We go looking for love and so often find fear
I have loved so many yet have lost them in
The swirling reflections of time and space
Their images stretched in all directions
With little sign of the one, I put my trust in

Sometimes I feel that it takes reaching with
The hand of God through this eternal land
Just to touch another soul
It doesn't take much to break a tender heart
Especially when the lover has
Brought with him
The shattered pieces of his life

With such brokenness we would do better
To gather ourselves in the arms of Love
But the carnival lures us in
And we can't help our want of distractions
Our appetite for such mad fancy
Surpasses our need to look into
The eye of another and say
"I love you, I See you
I may not fully understand you
But I will try to
Forgive my insensitivities
Sometimes I do not know how to speak
But please dear,
Try to remember my true face through the
Shattered fragments that seem to mirror
Everything but the truth of who we are

I am the face of God my love
May I remember that you are too"

The Devil Laughs

We stand above each other
Howling out our arrogance
We stand below in despair
When will we stand together?
The Devil laughs
At our lack of faith in each other

Some say it is all illusion
Your fear, your sorrow, your pain
Even if it's true that this is all a game
Grappling with your opponent
Was what led you to the win
And God only knows
You needed to win your life
To fully live your life
Sometime before the end

Take the Devil by the shoulders
And shake him good
Look him in the eye
Let him fuel the fire of your warrior's spirit
With the wit and will of those thousand heroes
Who went the course before

Laugh with him until he laughs no more
Till only your laughter is heard
Then let him be silenced by your reserve
Knowing you won with love

One More Mission

Inspiration is there when
The body is a willing participant
When a certain age arrives
So does a certain battle
With downward energy
It's a little like trying to keep
A star from collapsing
When it is on its way out

No doubt, one needs the bigger force
The one that comes from source
That is if we are to stay alive before we die

Every day I call upon you inner chi
Divine one who keeps the flame burning
The one who says there is more expression
To breathe through you
Another poem ready for the projection
Of spirit and soul
Another blank canvas asking for form
There is one more story to give its proper due

Perhaps the calling never dies
For there is always
One more mission left in you

Freedom

Freedom
You appear to us in many ways
As we try to wear your wings
Our whole life long
And fall time and again from your Grace
We try you on and try you out
Yet still wonder who you are

We ask, "Are you the sound of a child's
Laughter abandoned in joyous play?
Are you the rush of running nakedly
And winning at the running game?
Are you the one who howls at the moon
Your grievances and passions alike?
Or are you the one who takes this World
By storm in the middle of the night?"

We come in free spirits only to be confined
By the laws of Man
And the dogma of the Church
The many limits we put upon
Our Human potential
And those we put upon our Soul
It would seem, paradoxically
That the Ultimate imprisonment of
Mankind's Freedom is indeed
Mankind himself
Whose Ego stands at the Prison Gate
Having locked himself up
And thrown away the key

Freedom
You are the Soul's salvation
You are the arrow of its intent
You are the courage to face all obstacles
And the verve to stand for Truth
And beyond all, the Greatest Love
For only with Freedom can one be
Human enough to give
One's most vulnerable Heart

Freedom
You are the One daring enough to
Break down your Prison walls
And build a new order for the World

We have come a long way in Freedom's name
But the time has come to release our Soul
For True Peace from deep within

Surrender

*O*ur strivings,
Come the end, might all have been
Just more distraction from the True life
We might have lived sooner than later

Our greater good
Our actualization
Had to wait patiently
For a little stillness

Perhaps it was the darker friend that
Pushed us closer to the shining of our Soul
And the laughter, just within
Was waiting for its opening

There is a fertile territory in the
Otherness of our being
And consciousness waits to be
Born over and over again
When the time is right
This is how we grow the World

I live in the moment
And this moment is my Home
But it is so fleeting that sometimes I feel
Like a Homeless Vagabond
Looking for the next anchor to latch on to

No one cares to drift at sea
We need to feel the ground beneath our feet
To know where we are headed
But we are subject to the changing winds
For the moment we belong to
Will inevitably become the next
And we must keep up if we are
To keep in the rhythm of our life

Perhaps the Mystery is forever telling us
To forget about security
Forget about control
And fly like the birds
Who navigate on instinct
With a life force that keeps them
On their course
And makes the journey a simple joyous task
But it seems we Humans were born to worry
To measure each step of the way
As if the future would not come
Without forcing it

Where is Home, we ask
And where do we belong
Perhaps the answer lies
Somewhere within surrender
Where Freedom Is our Home

Grieving

When I was a child, I wanted to be alone
Already mourning the impending
Death of my mother

This became a way of life
In a lifetime of grieving
This was my pattern
A pattern for a quiet one
Wanting solitude yet company all at once

Perhaps this is the way of all grievers
In mourning for something Greater
For the One we lost when we were born
And the One we seek our whole life long

There is a Universal grieving
We all inevitably share
For the loss of our Mothers
Fathers, Ancestors and Friends
For the parts of ourselves
That die with each moment

Glimpses of memories are what remain
When the image in the mirror
Is unrecognizable
When beauty and youth are gone

Everything is stripped
From one's life eventually
And perhaps it's meant to be
That we may learn surrender

For if we resist the stripping away
We live and we die without knowing
The Truth of what it was about
Our Purpose...Our Essence
Our Meaning......Our Soul

What Does the Universe Want from Me?

What does the Universe want from me?
To hold a candle in the dark and illuminate
What could not be seen
What would not be seen
To hold a pic in the minds of men
To get to Soul
To get to Truth
To chisel away at the Rock of Ages
Containing the living beauty within
To crack the nut of Life
Of mine and of yours
I guess I don't care
How dirty I get in the process
If trouble is what it takes to get to the Center
I am an advocate for trouble
If chaos had to be entered into
In order to find order
Then you will find me there
Hanging by a single thread
Over the abyss
I may be a Sensitive in the light of day
But there is much to life
That needs the inner goods
And I guess I was born to this work
I am coming back with Eternity
A chunk of world Soul that time and again
Gets forgotten by the puppet world

Oh I know the game
I'm no different than you
You will find me well dressed
In my Sunday best
Gorging on this mockup life
You know, we want and want
But we don't know what we really want
So we buy it all and we buy it up
But there's never enough of this puppet stuff
I've had my fill of what cannot fulfill
So weary as I am and nearing the end
I am going in one more time
I'm heading in for the Immortal Soul
The one with whom I fell
Deeply and eternally in love
The one who partnered with Eros himself
And birthed the Child called Joy
This is how the story goes
Such love cannot be bought or sold
Such joy cannot be measured
When I die my fellow man
I pray I will walk hand-in-hand
With my Immortal Soul
And with my last breath
Thank God for the true Life I led

The Masterpiece

The Heart of humanity
Broken and fractured becomes humbled
Yet so full of longing that it grows
In yearning for your embrace
Perhaps it is the quake that carves
The way to your light

We enter the World
We travel everywhere to find the Center
To uncover the many secrets of life
And the Mysteries of the Universe

I was born into the arts
And came from a long line
Of painters, writers, opera singers
And even vaudevillians

I spent hours as a child
Listening to classical music
Imagining great ballets
I created a Grand puppet theater
And performed for invisible audiences
I would sit for hours looking up at the sky
Pondering the essence of God and Infinity

Already with a Mythic sense
I sang, I wrote, I painted, I performed

Did it serve as an escape
From my childhood tragedy?
They say the Soul's code is set long before birth
In my case crisis pushed me
Deeper into my Soul
And I was lucky enough to find
The meaning of my life
Through the arts

My bliss remained constant through the years
While my mission seemed to grow
And asked of me to contemplate
Filling a much greater role
So much of our seeking leads us
To a Higher Purpose

But perhaps my hours spent
Imagining great ballets to symphonies
Were the baby steps that brought me
Just a little closer to
My part of this magnificent
Masterpiece

The Usher

You and I and all of humanity
Wait through infinite ages
We spin like dervishes running
From that place inside ourselves
That knows what is to come
Death's arms openly wait for us
Hauntingly, ghost like

Lonely, frightened, we forget our Divinity
Each breath we take could bring us closer to
The Holiness we were meant to experience
Instead we run from our fear and run from life
But out of our deepest connection
To our inner being
Our Aloneness and the Oneness
With all merges
And Death itself smiles like a loving Mother
Who has only wanted for her child
To feel life's glory

She says, *"I've been with you always in Spirit*
You saw me as the Angel of Death
Black and ghoulish
But I am the beginning as well
As the so-called end

I am your loving usher
Lay your head on my shoulder
There, there
Take my hand"

Will You Know Me?

Will you know me in the end?
When I am washed away from
The memory of family or of friend?
No more touch…..No more laughter
No more marking the Earth
But with the remains of this
Once Lover of Life
Now nestled for the Big Sleep
I, who have been an eternal Romantic
In the face of Life's tragedies
Will have to be silent once it is over
I suppose I'll just have to leave
Romance to the future generation
Will they make the World anew?
A World full of grace and understanding?
I will be there in the wooded Hills
Beneath the eternal sun
And I will be watching
What will become of my Soul
While my body merges with the Earth?
Will I pass and be no more
When once I held a creative urge
So powerful that one wonders
How such things could simply
Stop with the stopping of one's Heart
I see my Spirit up on that Hill
Standing tall amidst the trees
Singing my song on the breath of the wind
The song I sang my whole life long
And now I am the Song

Temple Dream

Ten years from today
All this may be little more than misty
Memories scattered on the sea
Like me
The ocean will receive the ash
Of a once substantial life
And will rock me on the water
Till I dissolve or fly with angel wings
To the home of my Soul

Home... a place I see in dreams
A place as changeable as my changeable spirit
But always alive with warmth and love
The portal to the inner and the outer

It's almost as if Home is an entity itself
With nurturing arms and Sacred space
As if Home is like some kind of Mother
Perhaps the Great Mother
Perhaps the One

Home is like a womb for creativity
And therefore fertile
One feels a sense of safety
Home is the container
For the good life
For the true life

And for the many facets
Of the essence of one's being
Home must be like a Great Mansion
For the all that we are
And have the potential to become

There are so many images
Lo these many years
Of homes which appeared
In a lifetime of dreams

In youth I dreamed of houses on stilts
Surrounded by thick rich forests
And of many with expanding interiors
With high beamed ceilings
And windows looking out to the sky

I dreamt dollhouse dreams
Being forced open by my own growing self
I suppose an expanding consciousness
Needing its larger architecture
To contain itself

Once I had a dream of an Italian villa
So picture perfect and oh so noble
That it seemed to me indeed
I must have had a lifetime there
A lush life....... A magnificent life

But the one that feels eternal
The Original Home I expect
I will return to one day
When all this slips away
Was the one of my Mosaic Temple
By the shores of some ancient river
My sense is it was the home
Of some original essence within me
That is equally eternal
That essence being the Goddess
Barefoot and forever robed
In silken whites and long hair
Flowing on the river breeze
The sun peeking through the tall willows
This essence is the Goddess
Of the Land and Sea
Coming home to her Temple
In the Temple Dream
I think sometimes this
Universal search for Home
Inevitably brings us here within
And the message of the Temple Dream
Is the essence of the Mystery
That we ourselves are everything

The Soul…. the Goddess
The Land and the Sea
The Willows…The Rivers
And the Spirit of all things

All gathered together forever more
Right here in our Temple Dreams

Acknowledgements

There are many I wish to thank, some of whom directly supported the making of this book. And there were many who have inspired my life. I wish to thank them all.

Let me begin:
Angela Treat Lyon, for all of her support through the design process for the front cover. I am honored to use the image of her magnificent sculpture, "Yule Mama". Angela creates original and contemporary paintings and stone sculpture. See more of her work at http://AngelaTreatLyonArt.com

I would also like to thank:
Lori Hansen who helped transcribe this material
My beautiful and supportive friends: Karen, Paul, Deb, Eugene, Wayne, Melissa, and Jane
My beautiful supportive family: Paul, Shane, Stefani and Evan
My extraordinary mentors: Paul J. Curtis and Jean Houston
And finally, those great ones who continue to inspire –all those who went the course before and made the world a better place for their having been here.